T0061724

SAY WHAT?

HOW WE COMMUNICATE

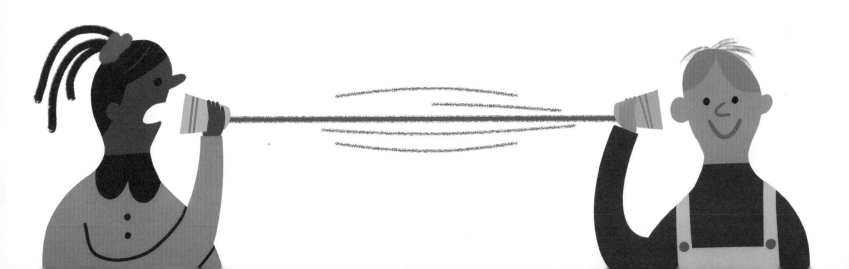

What is communication?

Communication is all about how we understand each other through our words and body language. You might think this happens naturally, and in a certain sense it does, but the ability to understand each other always depends on our abilities and skills. That's why it's good to think about how we communicate and try to improve our abilities. So let's get started!

In what ways do we communicate with others?

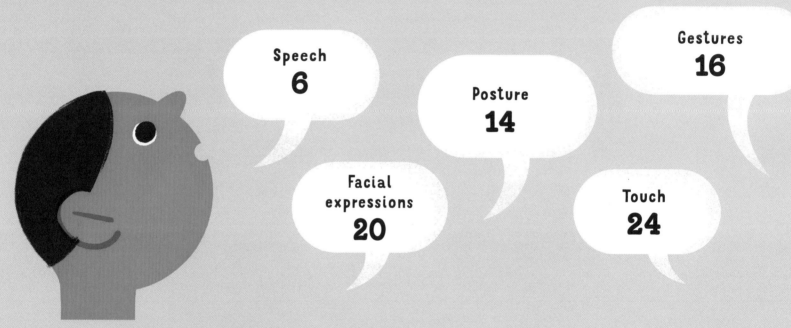

Speech
6

Posture
14

Gestures
16

Facial expressions
20

Touch
24

We humans have also developed ways to trade messages over long distances and pass information to future generations. What are they?

Symbols and signaling
28

Writing
30

There are also a few things that we need to consider when we're in contact with others, so that we can communicate well and understand each other better.

Communicating is important in all parts of our lives. Bad communicating can lead to bad things happening. But communicating well spreads hope and saves lives — and this will always be true. So, let's start by learning about some episodes in history when communication ended well and not so well.

Nowadays, we can also communicate with the aid of many new technologies.

Communication and us

One of the reasons is our ability to communicate and work together. Of course, some of us prefer peace and quiet now and then, but as a species, we humans are communicative creatures — meaning we love communicating. And this is probably why humans got so smart in the first place.

The way we communicate influences the people around us, and they in turn influence us.

We are constantly imitating the behavior of others, and most of the time we're not even aware of it.

We humans are equipped with a wonderful thing called **mirror neurons**. These are the cells in our brain that allow us to copy the behaviour of others. This is incredibly useful, because we learn and strengthen our relationships through imitating each other.

How we learn to communicate

From the moment we're born — and even before — we humans can communicate. When we're in the womb, we communicate with our mother mostly through touch. Once we are born, we come into contact with other people.

The best way of developing our communication skills is through play.

 SPEECH

 **RELATIONSHIPS**

LEARNING

	SPEECH	RELATIONSHIPS	LEARNING
0 years	Infants make noises and cry to show they don't like something.	Infants also maintain eye contact. A parent's touch and voice calms them best.	Their sight is not yet fully developed, so they react more to sounds and touch.
1 year	One-year-olds begin to say their first words.	They also mimic their parents' behavior and use simple gestures.	And they can name frequently used things.
2 years	Two-year-olds can speak in short sentences of a few words.	They can also use a wider variety of gestures and point to things. They notice when somebody else is crying.	And they can answer simple questions and know the names of people close to them.
3 years	Three-year-olds create longer and more complex sentences and can handle simple conversations.	They also imitate adults and friends and engage in play with other children.	And they can follow simple instructions and recognize colors.
5 years	Five-year-olds can tell a story and put their thoughts and opinions into words.	They also know how to cooperate and want to please their loved ones.	And they begin to recognize and write letters and numbers. They can also write their name.

Speech

Humans are not the only creatures that use their voices to communicate. Far from it — animals are able to communicate in a wide variety of ways too.

Dolphins communicate with whines and whistles.

Crickets chirp to communicate.

Birds communicate by singing.

> But human speech is truly unique.

How speech happens

In the first step, air is pushed out of the lungs. The air passes through the windpipe and acts as the motor of our voice. The sound itself is produced by the vocal cords. As the muscles contract and relax, the opening between the vocal cords widens and narrows. When combined with the air flow, this creates sound.

Now we have to process and shape this sound to transform it into words. This is called **articulation** and we do it with our lips, tongue, and the roof of our mouth.

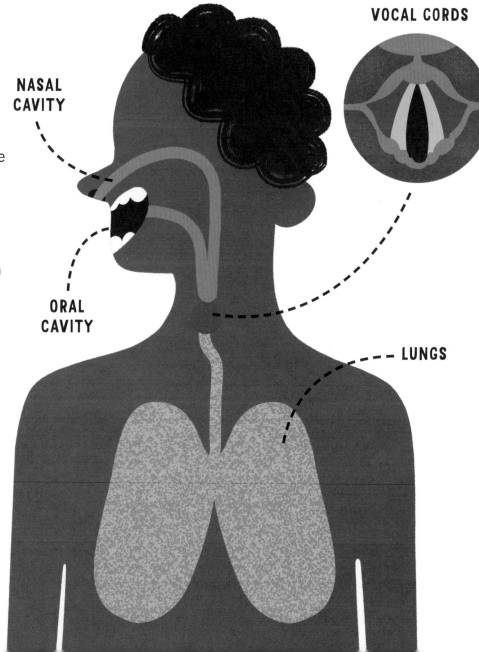

VOCAL CORDS

NASAL CAVITY

ORAL CAVITY

LUNGS

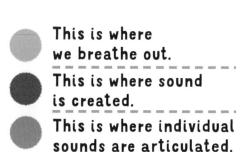

This is where we breathe out.

This is where sound is created.

This is where individual sounds are articulated.

How do we understand one another?

In order to communicate, we need to be able to understand one other. And our brain is perfectly equipped for this. As soon as we hear the beginning of a word, our brain offers us many different possible meanings. As the word continues, our brain rejects those meanings that don't make sense until it is left with the speaker's intended meaning. And it does all this in a fraction of a second!

What do we use our voice for?

screaming

making sounds

telling stories

singing

whispering

How do new words appear?

The language we speak is constantly changing. It evolves as people use it. Some words die out, while new ones keep appearing.

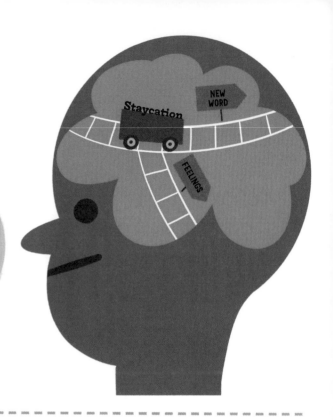

We often take words from other languages ...

... we combine existing words to create new ones ...

... or we change the meanings of words that already exist.

Foreign languages

There are over 7,000 different languages in the world. When we learn a new language, we also learn about the culture of the country that speaks it, thereby gaining a better understanding of the world. When humans first evolved, there were far fewer languages. But as people wandered the world and settled in new places, new languages developed.

Our voice

Intonation is where our voice falls and rises.

Volume is how **LOUDLY** or quietly we speak.

Speech tempo ishowquicklywespeak.

Articulation. Is. How. We. Form. Individual. Words.

Famous speakers

Our use of language gives us great power. Words can please or hurt people, they can change a person's mind, and they can even shape history. The art of speaking is called **rhetoric**. This page shows how speech was used by people whose words and rhetorical skills have endured across time.

> I saw injustice and I raised my voice for every girl's right to go to school.

Malala Yousafzai
(born 1997)
human rights activist and the youngest holder of the Nobel Peace Prize

> The difficulty, my friends, is not to avoid death, but to avoid unrighteousness ...

> I yearn for heart friendship between the Hindus, the Sikhs, and the Muslims.

Mahátma Gándhi
(1869–1948)
leader of the Indian independence movement

Socrates
(470–399 BCE)
Greek philosopher

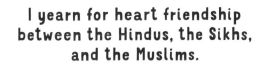

> I have a dream that my four little children will one day live in a nation where they will not be judged by the color of their skin but by the content of their character.

> The eyes of all future generations are upon you.

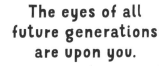

Greta Thunberg
(born 2003)
Swedish environmental activist

Martin Luther King
(1929–1968)
American leader of the Civil Rights Movement

9

To hear ...

A conversation is not just about telling the other person what you want them to know. It is just as important to understand what the other person is saying.

When I actively listen to another person, I pay full attention to what they're saying and I watch their body language. I don't judge them — I try to understand them.

... or to listen?

Silence

Silence is an incredibly useful thing. Silence gives us time and silence also builds tension. Films and theater would not work without silence. But did you know that there are different kinds of silence?

silence when there is no need to speak

comforting silence

angry silence

awkward silence

silence that gives us time to think

A story without words

Now we know that silence plays an important role in communication. But how do we convey information without speaking?

In fact, speech is not the most important part of communication. More than half of a message consists of what we call **non-verbal communication** — the things we express with our posture, facial expressions, and gestures.

Non-verbal communication allows us to understand each other without words. We all know how to do it. Let's see if you can describe what is happening in the following story.

If we needed words to communicate, we wouldn't be able to perform pantomime!

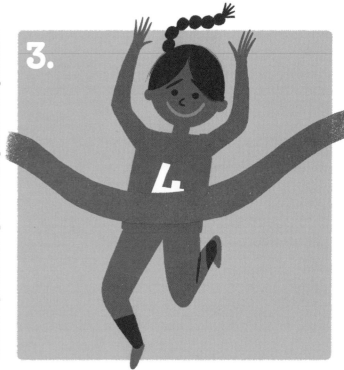

3.

5.

6.

7.

8.

Posture

I find you interesting.

E ven from a ways off, we can tell how a person is feeling, just by looking at the way they are standing. Are they standing straight up or are they slouching? Are their arms folded? Where are they looking – up or down? Our posture can convey many different feelings.

I'm happy.

I'm offended.

I'm angry.

I'm sad.

I'm nervous.

I'm having a good time.

I don't want to be noticed.

Our distance from another person

It is not only the way we stand that is important, but also how far away we stand from a person. It's no coincidence that we sometimes use the phrase "letting somebody get close to us." We tend to let our loved ones get closer to us than people we meet for the first time.

Different people, different distances

We all have our own **zone of personal space**. This is how close to us we allow others to come.

Each person's zone of personal space is different, and there's nothing wrong with that. It can look like this:

When a person enters our personal space and it makes us feel uncomfortable, it's okay to say:

That's a little too close for me. Could you move back a bit.

INTIMATE — family

PERSONAL — friends

SOCIAL — our teacher

PUBLIC — people in shops

ZONE

Gestures

We use gestures for non-verbal communication, but we also use them when we're speaking. Why is this? Why are gestures so important?

They help us communicate in situations where there's a language barrier.

They reinforce the information in our message and give it emphasis.

"Thank you" in American sign language

They help us when we're learning new things.

As with spoken language, sign language isn't universal. Different nations have different sign languages.

Showing your hands

Why are our hands so important? It's because they have more connections to our brains (a kind of connection called a *nerve connection*) than any other part of our bodies. Down through the ages, it has been important to see another person's hands to make sure they're not holding a weapon. That's why, even today, when a person hides their hands behind their back, it can make us feel pretty uneasy. We can't help but wonder what they're doing with them.

Well-known gestures

It's important to pay attention to the meaning of individual gestures, as a particular gesture may have different meanings for different nationalities or groups of people. A gesture that is normal in one society may offend people in another.

THUMBS UP
"I like it"

THUMBS DOWN
"I don't like it."

FINGERS ON LIPS
"Be quiet!"

WAVING
"Hello there!"

RAISED PALM FACING ANOTHER PERSON
"Stop!"

CLAPPING
"Well done!"

MAKING A CIRCLE WITH INDEX FINGER AND THUMB
"Okay, it's good!"

MOVING INDEX FINGER TOWARDS YOURSELF
"Come here!"

Let's swim up to the surface quick!

You should know the gestures for your particular environment!

It's all good. I'm enjoying it down here.

What to be careful about

Our bodies are very clever and very good at communicating non-verbally, even when we're not consciously controlling them. Still, sometimes it is useful to think about certain things that can hinder understanding.

When our body language doesn't match what we're saying with words, it confuses the listener!

Facial expressions

In this respect, we humans are unique — no animal can make as many expressions as we can.

Our faces are extremely versatile. They laugh, cry, frown, grimace, and so much more. There are a whole range of different expressions that reveal a lot about how we're feeling. Some of them look like this:

joy

surprise

fear

anger

sadness

disgust

These 6 feelings are universal — which means that even a person from another culture can guess your emotion from your expression.

Facial muscles

What is it that allows us to change our expressions and create so many of them? The answer is the muscles in our face. They allow us to change our expression in seconds.

What do facial muscles do?

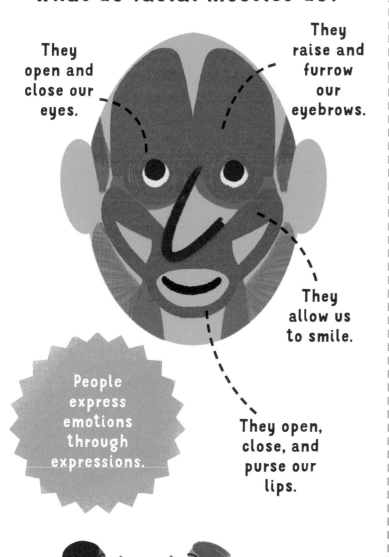

They open and close our eyes.

They raise and furrow our eyebrows.

They allow us to smile.

They open, close, and purse our lips.

People express emotions through expressions.

Facial expressions that we use

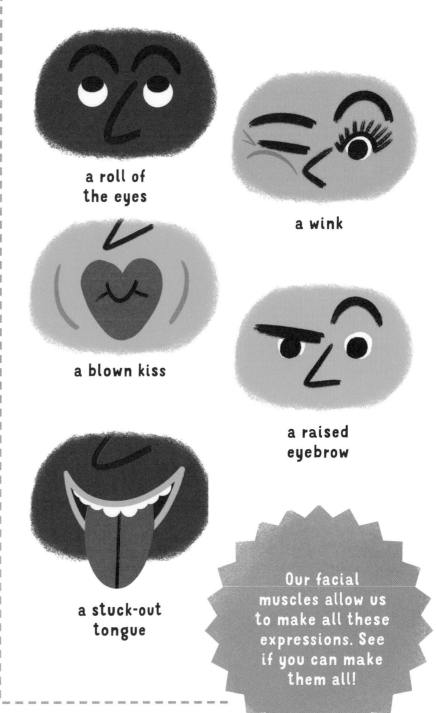

a roll of the eyes

a wink

a blown kiss

a raised eyebrow

a stuck-out tongue

Our facial muscles allow us to make all these expressions. See if you can make them all!

Look me in the eye

Eye contact is essential for communication. It shows that we're interested and allows us to read the other person's body language. It is also easier to trust people who look us in the eye. But be careful not to stare at anyone too long — this can make them feel very uncomfortable.

Crying

Sometimes we think of crying as something bad. But, in fact, it is extremely useful, as is laughter.

The tears we get when we cry are different than those we get when, for example, we poke ourselves in the eye. These emotional tears help us release the strong emotions that we're experiencing.

Crying plays an important role in communication. It lets others know that something out of the ordinary is happening.

We often feel relieved when we've had a really good cry.

Laughing

Our laughter is much closer to the sounds made by other animals than to human speech, which is more complex and evolved later.

Laughter helps strengthen relationships and improves our health and mood.

Although we all laugh differently, the process is the same for all of us. We make repeated short sounds that come from air being expelled from our body.

23

Touch

All humans need to touch — without it, we suffer both physically and mentally. On the other hand, frequent touching, hugging, and stroking works wonders for our sense of well-being. In short, the human body likes to be touched!

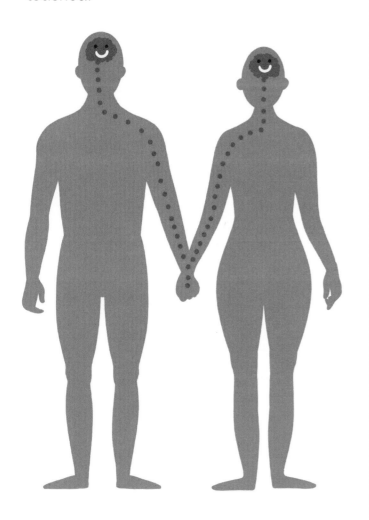

The moment we touch someone, information about that touch travels from that place to the brain. If the touch is pleasant for us, the brain is elated and starts to release a substance called **oxytocin**, which gives us a nice feeling.

Our sense organ of touch is our skin, which is also our body's largest organ. Parts that are very sensitive to touch are:

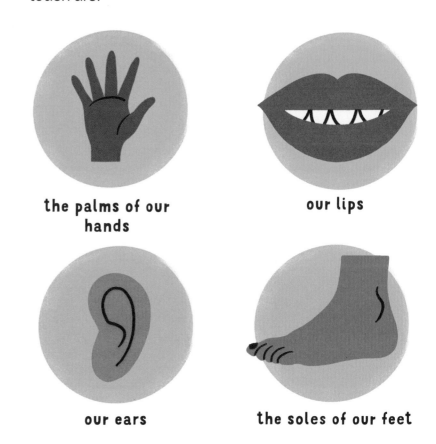

the palms of our hands

our lips

our ears

the soles of our feet

Touching can be pleasant or unpleasant for us. What is pleasant for one person may be quite unpleasant for another.

Remember, it is never okay to hurt another person!

How we touch

KISSING
"I love you!"

**TAPPING SOMEBODY'S
SHOULDER**
"Can I have your
attention?"

**PATTING SOMEBODY
ON THE BACK**
"Well done!"

HUGGING
"I'm so happy to see you!"

CLAPPING
"That's wonderful!"

SHAKING HANDS
"Pleased to meet you."

**PUTTING AN ARM AROUND
SOMEBODY'S SHOULDER**
"I'm here for you."

Interacting with
people by touch
is sometimes
called **haptic
communication**.

Reading by touch

For some people, touch can
substitute for other methods of
communication. For example,
visually impaired people can read
books written in **Braille**. In this
system of writing, each letter is
made up of differently arranged
dots that stick out of the surface
of the paper and thus can be
distinguished from the others
by touch.

We all need to communicate

Now you know that we communicate with the people around us in many different ways. But can you imagine what it's like to not be around other people and to have no contact with them? This was the experience of a girl named Helen Keller.

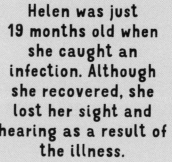

In 1870, in Alabama, a healthy little girl was born named Helen.

Helen was just 19 months old when she caught an infection. Although she recovered, she lost her sight and hearing as a result of the illness.

Because Helen couldn't hear other people speaking, she didn't learn to speak herself. She was cut off from all people, with no way of communicating other than touch. Her whole world was dark and silent.

Helen became an unruly child. She knew that other people communicated with each other in ways she didn't understand. She often had fits of rage and hurt other people.

Helen learned to read Braille and even to speak. When she placed her hand on another person's face, she could make out the movements of their mouth and understand what they were saying.

With empathy and incredible patience, Anne explained to Helen that all things had names. She taught her the letters of the alphabet by touching the palm of her hand.

With Anne's help, Helen became the first deaf-blind person to graduate from university. She learned foreign languages and studied literature, history, and mathematics.

Helen wrote books and magazine articles and gave lectures advocating for the visually impaired, fighting racism, and struggling for women's equality.

One day, a young teacher named Anne Sullivan came to join the family. Helen later remembered this meeting as the most important day of her life.

Anne remained with Helen until she died. Throughout her life, she had helped Helen to understand the world around her.

Symbols

Even before our ancestors invented writing, they were able to communicate different kinds of information by using simple symbols. Meaningful symbols used for communication even appear in prehistoric cave paintings.

Nowadays, we also communicate with various pictures and signs. These symbols represent real things. If you think that's difficult to imagine, see if you can understand some of these symbols:

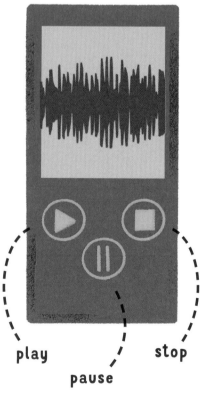

play   stop

pause

red and green
man traffic signs

sign
for danger

flag

arrows
showing direction

Some symbols and signals are only known by a certain group of people. These are extremely useful for secret messages.

Signaling

Although symbols carry a certain meaning, it is difficult to convey a complex message with them. That's why people use lots of kinds of signals. These are often light or sound signals.

Dots and dashes

Morse code is perfect for signaling. In this code, all letters are converted into dots and dashes that can be heard on special radios (originally it was used in an older technology called the telegraph). This means we can send any message we like.

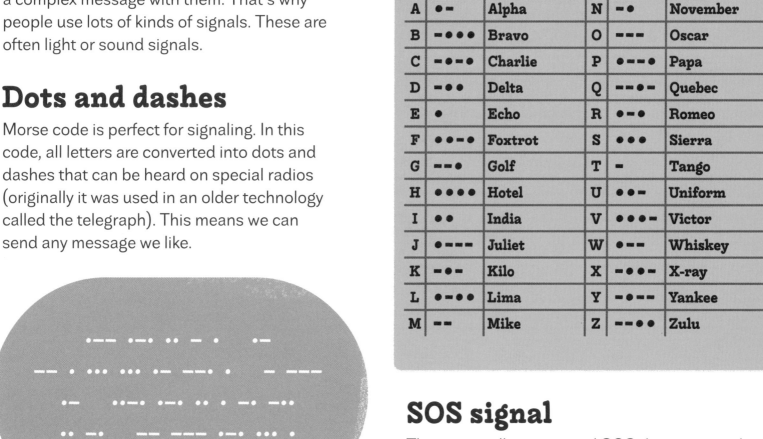

A	•–	Alpha	N	–•	November
B	–•••	Bravo	O	–––	Oscar
C	–•–•	Charlie	P	•––•	Papa
D	–••	Delta	Q	––•–	Quebec
E	•	Echo	R	•–•	Romeo
F	••–•	Foxtrot	S	•••	Sierra
G	––•	Golf	T	–	Tango
H	••••	Hotel	U	••–	Uniform
I	••	India	V	•••–	Victor
J	•–––	Juliet	W	•––	Whiskey
K	–•–	Kilo	X	–••–	X-ray
L	•–••	Lima	Y	–•––	Yankee
M	––	Mike	Z	––••	Zulu

Samuel Morse

SOS signal

The universally recognized SOS distress signal was specifically created for Morse code. If you ever found yourself in a life-or-death situation, you could use this signal to call for help.

Writing

The very first writing consisted of simple signs and pictures of things. Gradually, these symbols became simpler and were used to describe non-material things, until we arrived at the script we use today. In the beginning, it was mostly used for keeping financial records and trade.

What is written must be true!

Evolution of writing

One of the earliest examples of writing is the **cuneiform script** from Ancient Mesopotamia. The text was carved into clay tablets with reeds.

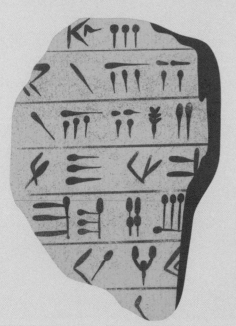

Egyptian **hieroglyphs** came a little later. First they were carved in stone and then they were written on papyrus.

In the Middle Ages, the Church was primarily responsible for the spread of writing. The text was written mostly with a quill pen on thin wooden boards or parchment made from animal skin.

Writing began to develop separately in various places in the world at the same time. And it was a very useful thing. Thanks to writing, we can store information for many years or send it over long distances.

The most widely used writing system is the Latin (aka Roman) script. In fact, that's what this book is written in it. Just as there are different languages, there are also different alphabets. For example, in addition to Latin, there are the Cyrillic and Arabic alphabets.

In 1448, Johannes Gutenberg invented the **printing press**. This made it possible to print a large amount of text at once and produce many copies.

In the second half of the 19th century, the **typewriter** was invented. Typing was faster than writing with a pen and it was easier to read the results.

Book printing marked a fundamental breakthrough in the spread of information and knowledge.

Nowadays, we use different kinds of technological devices for writing, such as computers, cell phones, and tablets.

31

Written messages – past and present

messenger

message board

letters

books

 message in a bottle

person-to-person

writing on walls

text
messages

fax

pigeon
post

information
signs

social media

newspapers

e-mails

Mass communication

Throughout the 20th century, there was incredible development in mass communication — that is, the ability to reach many people. At first, it was through radio and printed newspapers. Then came television broadcasting and finally internet communication.

1912
The "unsinkable" ship the *Titanic* sinks. (p. 46)

1913
Richard Platz throws a message in a bottle into the sea, in which he asks the finder to return the message to his address.

1908
SOS becomes an internationally recognized signal. (p. 29)

1904
Helen Keller graduates from university. (p. 26)

1906
The first radio voice broadcast in history.

1982
The first ever use of an emoticon. :-)

1992
Discovery of mirror neurons. (p. 4)

1991
Launch of the World Wide Web. (p. 38)

2004
Facebook is launched.

The first SMS text message in history is sent.

1997
Human rights activist Malala Yousafzai is born (p. 9)

1998
Google is launched.

1928
First public television broadcast.

1936
In England, the BBC launches the world's first regular public television service. The first broadcast included the song "Television", celebrating the new technology.

1939–1945
World War II

1954
Production begins on the first color television set available to the public.

1914–1918
World War I

1969
First Moon landing. (p. 47)

1971
The first ever e-mail is sent.

ARPANET is created, the forerunner of the Internet.

1963
Martin Luther King delivers his famous "I Have a Dream" speech. (p. 9)

2005
YouTube is launched.

Dancing cat

2014
Richard Platz's message in a bottle is found and shown to his granddaughter.

2016
TikTok is launched.

The Telephone

Telephones make our lives so much easier. They allow us to talk or send messages to a friend from pretty much anywhere. We can also use phones to watch and record videos, play games, shop, and take photos.

Alexander Graham Bell is generally considered to be the inventor of the telephone. However, some people believe his invention was not the first and claim that the telephone was invented not by an American but by an Italian named Antonio Meucci.

ALEXANDER GRAHAM BELL

INVENTOR OF THE TELEPHONE

Antonio Meucci

What happens when you call a friend?

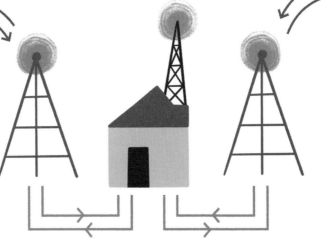

2.
But as these waves cannot travel great distances, they need a little help. This is what transmitters are for. The transmitter receives your wave signal and sends it through underground optical fibers to the transmitter closest to your friend.

1.
Your phone converts your voice into a simple code. It then sends this signal in the form of invisible electromagnetic waves.

3.
This transmitter converts the signal back into waves and sends it to your friend's phone. There, these waves are converted back into voice.

Development of the telephone

The smartphones of today have come a long way since Alexander Bell's invention.

1930s
Desktop telephone with rotary dial

Turn of the 20th century
"Candlestick" telephone

1970s
Wall telephone

1960s
Desktop telephone with push button dial

1983
The world's first mobile phone

1980s
Cordless desktop telephone

The first phone with a color display (1997) had only four colors.

Turn of the 21st century
Cell phones become small enough to fit in your pocket.

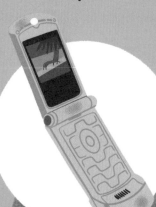

2007
The first iPhone became the model for all later smartphones.

1990s
New mobile phone models appear with a display.

Flip phones are all the rage.

The Internet

The Internet is something we use every day – without giving it much thought. It allows us to do a lot of great things like making video calls to friends halfway around the world, playing games, and sending photos and e-mails.

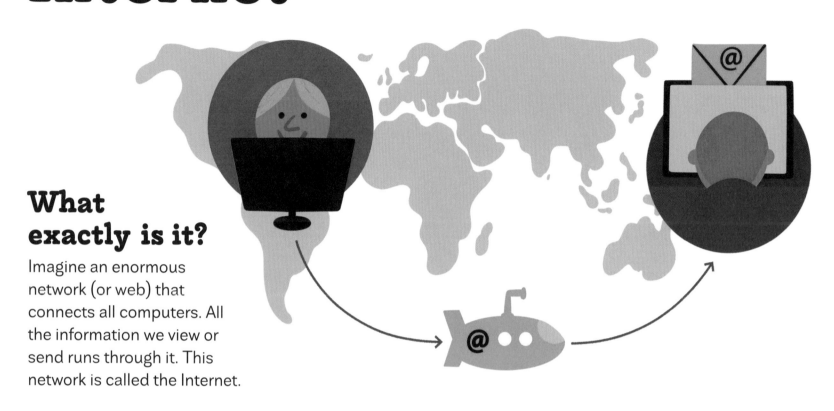

What exactly is it?

Imagine an enormous network (or web) that connects all computers. All the information we view or send runs through it. This network is called the Internet.

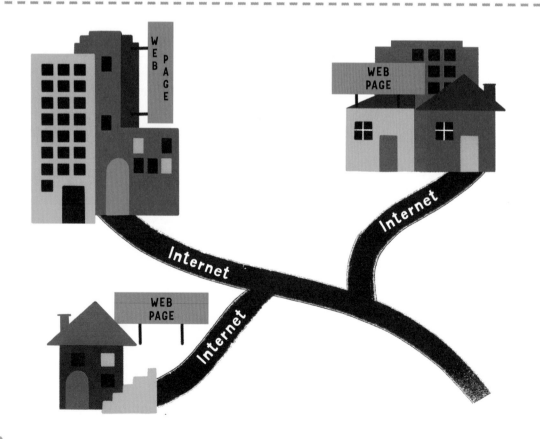

The Web or the Internet?

This may come as a surprise, but they are not the same thing. The World Wide Web is a network of websites with different content, which you search for using browsers. You can imagine it like this: The Internet is a road that connects different cities, whereas websites are buildings and other objects that are found along the road.

Netiquette

Let's take a look at the rules of appropriate behavior in the online world:

RESPECT THE PRIVACY OF OTHERS.

Always remember that some people don't like it when you share their personal information. For example, some people don't want to be tagged in photographs that everybody can see.

IF YOU WOULDN'T SAY SOMETHING TO THE OTHER PERSON'S FACE, YOU SHOULDN'T SAY IT OVER THE INTERNET.

Always keep in mind that there is a person sitting at the other end who may be hurt by your remark, even if it is well intentioned.

MAKE SURE YOUR INFO IS CORRECT BEFORE YOU SHARE IT.

There is a lot of false and misleading information on the Internet. So before you share anything, make sure you're not spreading lies or misleading information.

For more info, check out: beinternetawesome.withgoogle.com

EXPRESS YOURSELF CLEARLY, POLITELY, AND RESPECTFULLY.

Don't forget to read your message thoroughly before you send it, so you can avoid mistakes and misunderstandings. You may have a particular way of communicating with your friends, but it may not be OK for communicating with others.

Beward the trolls!

Remember that there are also people on the Internet who hide behind fake accounts. Their aim is to spread false information, attack other people, and sow hatred. You could think of them as cruel trolls, which is what we call them. The best response to them, though, is to not respond at all. As people say online: "Don't feed the trolls."

Staying safe when communicating

Sometimes we may not feel comfortable communicating with another person. It could be that something is happening that is not okay. Here are a few tips on how to behave.

> I was looking forward to us playing together, and now I'm disappointed that you don't want to.

> I know what's going on inside me and I can say what's the matter.

> That's enough, Grandma. You can stop now.

> ... and this is where we keep the spare key!

I can say "I don't like it, please stop!" when I don't like what's happening to me.

Sometimes I need some quiet time to myself. And when I need it, I do what I can to get it.

I don't have to tell another person everything about myself. Sometimes, it's better to keep certain things to ourselves.

UNTRUE RUMORS ARE SPREADING ABOUT A NEW, EXTRA DELICIOUS ICE CREAM FLAVOR.

> Did you know they're now selling new extra delicious ice cream there?

ICE CREAM

SCOOP $2

> Could I have one of your new extra delicious ice creams, please!

I think critically. When people tell me things, I ask: Where did this information come from? How do I know it's true? What do people I trust, such as my parents or my teacher, say about it?

Staying safe online

Since virtually all of us do things online these days, it is useful to learn a few rules, so that this form of communication is also safe for us.

These rules don't cover everything. It's important to talk to your parents and work out together what else you need to do or avoid.

Remember, the **Internet doesn't forget!** Whatever you share will, from then on, be available online forever. Furthermore, **nothing you send is truly private.** Even messages from a private conversation may be seen by lots of other people.

Don't share your personal information or anything you wouldn't be willing to say or show in public.

Never meet up in person with anybody you only know online.

Always use passwords and do not show them to anybody.

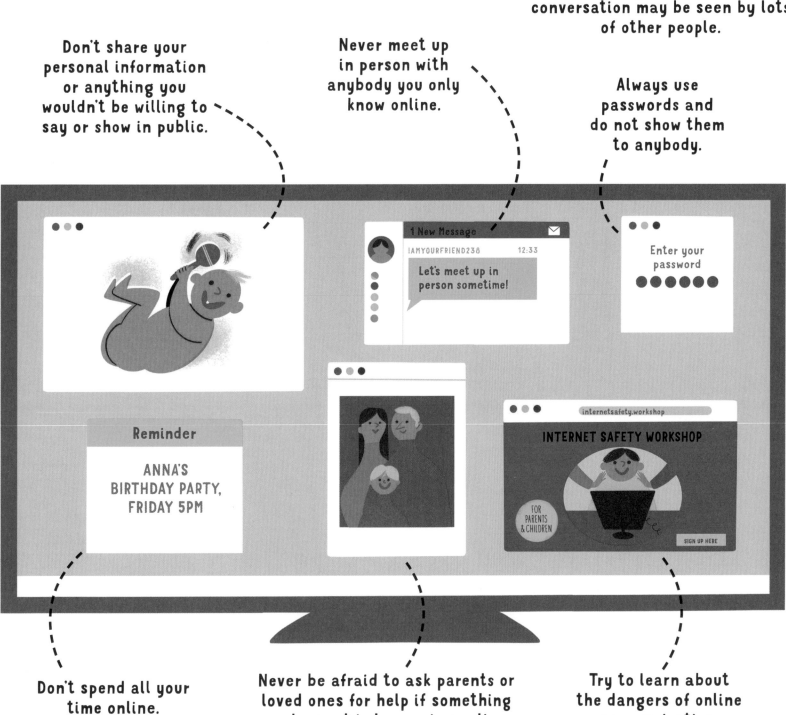

Don't spend all your time online.

Never be afraid to ask parents or loved ones for help if something unpleasant is happening online.

Try to learn about the dangers of online communication.

Useful things to know

Our behavior often shows how we actually feel. Our feelings can sometimes mess with our communication. Nevertheless, they are completely normal and natural. And it's much easier if we take them into account and know how to manage them.

Our feelings and **emotions**, such as joy, anger, and disappointment, are part of us. And they are ours alone. When faced with the same situation, two people may have completely different feelings. It is never wrong to feel a certain way. What is important is how we express our feelings.

> Now Mommy will pay me some attention!

NOT OKAY

> Come and play with me!

> I just have to finish something here. We can play together in five minutes.

OKAY

When we're able to name our feelings, we can explain them better to others. At the same time, we develop our ability to **empathize**, which is how we understand our own feelings and the feelings of others.

> Answer the following question: How do I feel at this moment?

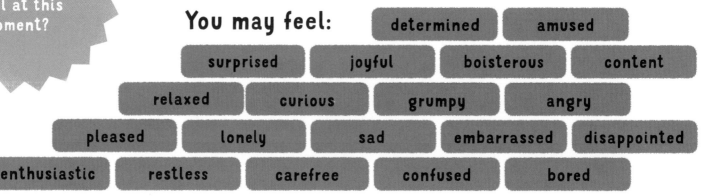

You may feel: determined · amused · surprised · joyful · boisterous · content · relaxed · curious · grumpy · angry · pleased · lonely · sad · embarrassed · disappointed · enthusiastic · restless · carefree · confused · bored

Conflicts

Sometimes, we get along with a person naturally. However, with some people, communication can be so difficult that we can't agree on anything. This is perfectly normal, although it can be very unpleasant.

WHAT IS CONFLICT?
Sometimes we simply can't agree on something with another person, because we both want something different.

FIRST STEP
Take a deep breath and be aware of how you feel.

DEALING WITH THE PROBLEM
- Say how you are feeling and ask the other person how they feel.

- Try not to judge the other person and make an effort to understand them.

- Work together to find a solution to the problem.

USEFUL THINGS TO BEAR IN MIND
- Conflicts are normal and happen all the time. It's how we deal with them that matters.

- Sometimes there isn't a solution that is good for both sides.

- It's not possible for us to clear up every misunderstanding.

WHY CONFLICTS ARE USEFUL
A conflict offers us an opportunity to resolve our disagreement with another person and improve our relationship.

Communication tips

We all have our own unique character. Some people will talk to anybody at the drop of a hat, while others prefer to keep to themselves. Even so, there are a few things it is useful for us all to know. If we do, we'll get along with everybody much better. Here's a short list:

accept responsibility for what you say and do

I'm sorry, I broke that vase ...

be ready to compromise

No, thanks. I'd like to read now.

speak your mind

be there for others and lend a sympathetic ear

Some of these things will come naturally, while others may be a little harder. But don't be afraid to try and don't worry about making mistakes. We learn through our mistakes.

Missed calls ...

1776

An unread message

In the Battle of Trenton, during the American Revolutionary War, Americans fought Germans hired by the British. German Commander Johann Rall had received a message from a spy warning him about a planned attack during the night. He took the note, put it in his pocket ... and forgot about it. The American attack surprised the Germans, who were defeated after a short battle. Rall died in the attack, with the unread note still in his pocket.

The sinking of the *Titanic*

Just seconds before the *Titanic* hit an iceberg, the radio operator on the nearest ship, the *Californian*, finished his duty and therefore did not hear the *Titanic's* distress call. The crew of the *Titanic* later fired flares, but the *Californian* did not understand them as distress signals. The sinking of the *Titanic* claimed more than 1,500 lives, and only 705 passengers survived. If the nearest ship had come to its aid, many more people could have been saved.

1999

The loss of a space probe

The Mars Climate Orbiter was sent to Mars to collect information about the Martian climate. But for reasons not known at the time, the probe came too close to the planet's atmosphere and burned up. It was later discovered that while the development team had used American units of measurement, the space agency's control center had used the metric system. This small communication error cost NASA a whopping $125 million dollars.

... and successes in communication

Winton's children

During World War II, Sir Nicholas Winton saved more than 650 Jewish children from almost certain death in Nazi concentration camps. Winton secured surrogate families and visas for the children and organized transportation. In all, eight trains left Prague taking the children to safety in London.

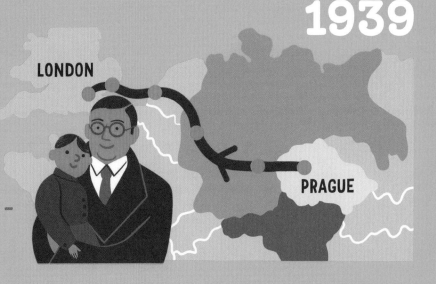

1939

LONDON

PRAGUE

That's one small step for man, one giant leap for mankind.

1969

The Moon landing

It was broadcast live on every radio and TV station in the world. Never before had so many people in the world gathered to watch a single event at the same time. The crew of Apollo 11 were in contact with Earth throughout the mission, so everybody could follow how it was going. For the first time in history, a person stepped on the surface of the moon ... and people on Earth were able to witness it!

2010

WE ARE OK

The Chilean mine collapse

In San José in Chile, a rock slide trapped 33 miners deep underground. Up on the surface, most people believed that it was unlikely that anybody had survived the accident. However, after 17 days, the miners managed to send a written message up on the head of the drill that was sent to find them. After that, food and equipment were sent down, but it still took 70 days in total to rescue them.

Scan the QR code for more information and sources.

© B4U Publishing for Albatros,
an imprint of Albatros Media Group, 2024
5. května 1746/22, Prague 4, Czech Republic
Written by Radka Píro
Illustrated by Charlotte Molas
Translated by Mark Worthington
Edited by Scott Alexander Jones

www.albatrosbooks.com

All rights reserved.

Reproduction of any content is strictly prohibited without the written permission of the rights holders.